PARIS
© **Les Editions du Pacifique** 1978
    10, avenue Bruat, Papeete - TAHITI
English language text copyright© Les éditions du Pacifique, 1978
All rights reserved
Published in 1978 by **The Vendome Press**
Distributed by **The Viking Press**
625 Madison Avenue, New York, N.Y. 10022
Published simultaneously in Canada by Penguin Books Canada, Ltd.
Library of Congress catalog card number: 78-19578
ISBN O-670-40976-6
Printed and bound in Japan by Zokeisha Publications, Ltd.
Set in France by Publications-Elysées

The joy of
PARIS

PHOTOGRAPHY
AND
DESIGN
BERNARD HERMANN
TEXT
EDITED BY
GEORGINA OLIVER
OF
"PARIS-METRO"

The Vendome Press
New York / Paris / Lausanne
Distributed by
The Viking Press

CONTENTS

Paris is...

Paris is... roof tops. Roof tops, but without the red balloon featured in Lamorisse's film swiftly, naively drifting above the capital's charismatic counterpoint of gray slate tiles, odd-sized chimneys and lace-curtained garret windows.

Paris is a dream city, where the mind drifts as easily as *péniches* barges slide up the Seine, imagining that cute little red balloon. Imagining sparrows conglomerating on the endless, leg-aching, steep, stone steps of Montmartre leading up to the Sacré-Cœur basilica. Cheerful sparrows clustered together like a group of agitators, or like so many suspicious *flics,* cops, cheerful in spite of their sinister black capes, that went out twenty years ago. Sparrows popularly know as "piaſs", from which the immortal Edith borrowed her singer's name.

In Paris, somewhere in those roof tops a star is born every day, for anything can happen in Paris. Elusive, enigmatic, Paris is the city of a million illusions, in which one imagines at least as much as one actually sees. Paris is an Alice-through-the-looking-glass city : a wonderous, frenzied place that lends itself to reflection, to contemplation. Strolling along the *Quai aux Fleurs,* through the flower and bird market, in summer one is almost overcome by the heady, heavy smell of manure and damp feathers. It is a whole scene. A whole trip.

The stuff dreams are made of

Bohemian. Monumental. Aware of the appeal of its traditions. Paris is an artist's haven, where absolute havebeens are rare. For long after a play-wright, singer, painter or author has become established to the point of seeming over-exposed, the Parisian public finds a place in its otherwise fickle heart for such legendary figures. Figures who remind them of how it felt to live, to work, to love, in their capital, at one particular point in time. Their time. Their youth. Creative minds are at once inspired and awe-inspired by Paris' intellectual prestige, while even the most blasé of visitors allows himself to be taken unaware by the special magnetism, which means that every one daydreams in Paris.

Let yourself go. Don't be afraid to be fanciful. Paris is the stuff dreams are made of. Set your imagination free. That is what Paris is there for. In Paris everything is "fou, fou, fou." Mad, wild, crazy. Dream a little of Paris. Close your eyes and pretend you don't know "real" Paris exists. Close your eyes and dream of that "other" Paris. It's an essential antidote to the aggressive bustle which makes Paris Paris. Start with a stereotype like Piaf.

Dream Paris is *Piafs* chirping *La vie en rose* out of tune, as an *ancien combattant* war veteran feeds them millet seed and dry bread. Those sparrows know him well. He comes to visit them every day. Wearing his navy blue *beret* at a slight slant. Carrying a crusty *baguette* of French bread. Proud that his legs can still carry him up those steep steps. Too proud to pin his impressive regalia of medals to his lapel. He keeps them tucked away, at home, in a mahogany drawer that has become hard to open. He keeps them folded inside a lavender scented handkerchief, side by side with a quaint *billet doux,* romantic postcard, that reads "Unis pour la vie" (together for ever) in ornate Art Nouveau lettering. That reminds him that he too was once a lover in Paris in the month of May, when lily-of-the-valley is sold on street corners to celebrate spring. On May 1st, a workers' holiday, Paris is for once truly carefree, sunny, light and breezy.

Even if "real Paris is like retirement-pace compared to the sti-moo-lation of New York" (ex-Parisian, now N.Y.C.—based painter Richard Lindner's rating), all agree that Paris remains an impassive, beautiful *femme fatale*. Elegant, but cruel. A star. Paris has come a long way since the days when she led a simple, natural existence, alone and aloof on the Ile de la Cité. Days when she answered to the Gallic name, Lutetia. And she knows it too. Paris has a hold on those who move into her enclave to look beyond the official facade. The military gear and uniforms. Superbly cut. Trimmed with white gloves. With white plumes. Refined to the last stitch and gilt button. Beyond the galloons and festoons. The festive, fair-ground candy floss of a city redoutable for its sense of sophistication and style.

A many-splendoured thing

Paris is the guards of the Elysée presidential palace impeccably turned out in apparel as smooth and studied as the luxury, ladies accessories sold opposite in Faubourg Saint Honoré's exclusive boutiques.

Paris is the military precision. The martial chic. Which *Parisiennes* of the ruling classes apply to their slick choice of clothing co-ordinates. Subdued, but dressed to kill...

The snobbish stiffness of the navy blue, pearls and poodle sixteenth arrondissement uniform is a dying breed, being supplanted slowly but surely by "new" conventional dress, by the sharp staccato of the made-to-measure riding boots, densely vertical silk pleated skirt, bushy, burly fur jacket, sports car and Scottish miniature dog brigade.

Paris is not the kind of dame you love and leave. Nor the kind of dame you love and forget. Don't call her. She will call you.

The gargoyles of Notre-Dame cathedral know all about Paris' coquettish antics. About the feigned disdain. The *décontracté*, casual condescension, with which she treats young suitors. Dream a little... Glistening in the rain, pathetic as bulldogs, those gargoyles pity the slow progress of a thin, underfed, aspiring playwright whom they have been watching. Hunched. Struggling against the cold, wet, biting wind. On the banks of the Seine. Long, knitted scarf, wildly, madly flying. Out of control. Frostbitten hands carrying his notes taken at the *Bibliothèque Forney* arts library. Kept in a battered leather music satchel, perhaps. But concerts or films he cannot afford. The refrain he has heard most lately is "Un Paris beurre—un", the order for his Paris ham sandwich meals, in cheap and dirty left bank bistros. Not Brasserie Lipp. Not Deux Magots.

Paris is a capital is a capital is a capital. An enthralling city. Magnetic as any other capital, where capital matters most and ordinary people just try to exist.

Facing the challenge

True Parisians rise to the challenge. That's what gives them their reputation for being aggressive. They have a long-cultivated talent for getting by. For managing to make it in the city where, to put it at its most pessimistic, all ideas are bad until proven otherwise. A mentality which has its roots in the strict master-pupil relationships which are part of the *lycée,* high school, atmosphere. Part of the highly competitive, wait-until-you're-asked-before-you-enquire, approach of the French educational system. A system that is regulated to the extent that until recently it was said that throughout France at any one time during the school year children studying in the same grade would be opening the same book at exactly the same page, at precisely the same moment.

Nowhere in France is this resistant, critical attitude more deeply engrained than in Paris. A schoolmasterly refusal to get the point of any idea that is original, individualistic or simply "new" greets many newcomers. Paradoxically, Parisians are individualistic, desperately so. For to break that barrier is to pierce a taut and tenuous membrane, to break through: "percer". "Percer" in Paris is "la gloire", glory, a heavyweight term with traditional connotations, Parisian for plain old success. Get your break in Paris and Maxim's becomes your canteen, instantly.

Nowhere in Paris is the maxim "chacun pour soi et Dieu pour tous" (Each for himself and God for all) applied more tenaciously than at the wheel. Paris is traffic: agressive, rude driving. A succession of sounds and flashing images: screeching brakes, angry headlights, hot-tempered horns. Punctuated by swearing and harsh, merciless assessments of fellow drivers' intelligences, rash and severe as a rap of the schoolmaster's rule across junior finger nails, numb with astonishment.

Paris is a permanent traffic jam. A tangle of vehicles, drivers and drivers' temperaments without which Paris would not be Paris, but there is more to Paris than postcard magic generated by the flickering neon-semaphore of motorized Paris-by-night taking an after dinner stroll round the Place de l'Etoile (Place Charles de Gaulle, since 1970).

Paris is bridges : Pont Alexandre III. Pont Marie. Domes, arches, boundless avenues. Places to walk. Places to reflect. Paris is a capital in which isolation can be the price of privacy. With romantic settings, that make a spell of spleen seem ten times more penetrating; and blues bluer.

In the cool light of the morning depending on who and where you are in Paris, you may wake up to the howl of shrieking factory sirens (stark, modern apartment block by one of the city's peripheral East/West/North/South speedways) or to a five-star, bi-lingual "room service, good morning. Vous désirez, Monsieur ?... Bacon and eggs or *café-complet* (continental breakfast)? We have both, Sir," (two star hotel, just off the Champs Elysées).

In Paris, however rested you may feel when you wake up, it is probable that by nightfall you will be a bundle of nerves.

The moveable feast

Whatever your location, zoom into central Paris and you soon realize that the city is a dizzy, bubbling champagne cocktail of fumes and perfumes, odors and fragrances. Because of this or in spite of it, Parisians are perhaps the most pollution, cancer and calory conscious of capital city dwellers. Checking into health food shops. Checking dates on yoghurt pots. Like maniacs. Never eating "fast food" with high carbohydrate contents or artificial flavors (except in front of friends, as punk posture). Forming weight-watcher's clubs and ecology committees, at the rate rabbits breed.

Parisians are community-conscious for big world issues but diabolically selfish in minor matters. In movie queues, in the subway, in the traffic: where the attitude is spartan, based on the survival of the fittest. Jungle law.

Paris at its most fume-ridden is the city's subway. The *métro*. Where social contrasts are more obvious than anywhere else in the capital. Paris has a cast system. First and second class *métro* carriages. First and second class citizens. Tight, closed Parisian circles. Entrenched. Cut-off from the popular, Parisian masses. From the vast, faceless crowd.

Paris is poverty. The *clochards,* bums, seek warmth on the *métro*'s benches, where they sleep, down litres of *vin ordinaire,* red wine, and unravel and repack the contents of apparently unfathomable, tatty, plastic bags, to count their possessions.

Unshaven *clochards.* Fighting. Sleeping and sleeping some more.

There are beggars in the subway. Children and gipsies. Students and buskers that sing Simon and Garfunkel, Dylan, Baez. Mutilated beggars exposing their stumps. Blind musicians. Blind lottery ticket vendors repeating in the same, constant, bewildering monotone: "J'ai des millions plein les poches. J'ai des millions plein les poches. J'ai des millions plein les poches." *I've got millions in my pockets* they just keep right on saying, eyes obscured by dark glasses, as if they were... waiting for Godot.

Parisians are as aggressively Parisian in the *métro* at peak hours as they are in the privacy of their own cars. Only in the *métro,* that same aggressiveness seems to be underplayed, understated, implied not unleashed. Frustrated. Contained. Parisians glare at each other in the *métro,* assessing one another's external appearances with suppressed hostility. Married? Unmarried? North African? Been to the hairdresser recently?

Underground city

In the *métro* women knit. Men read. Anything to avoid that glare. That Parisian stare that gives them an instant rating, like the grades they used to get at school. Above average. Below average. Any grade between 0 and 20. The pupils who got 16 1/2 had just the required edge over the next, those who were graded a mere 16.

In the *métro,* there are a number of seats reserved for pregnant women, persons accompanied by small children, the handicapped and war veterans. Those are grudgingly conceded. But it is rare that a Parisian *métro* user gets up from an isle seat and sits by the window to make room for a fresh arrival. First come, first served. It would be degrading to move: a true Parisian sparrow never yields territory.

The *métro* has a special smell. It gives off a curious Molotov mixture of pine and ammonia-scented detergent, stale *Gitanes* tobacco and filth, with the occasional unsavory reminder that there are sewers lurking behind the scenes.

Even in Paris' *beaux quartiers,* classy districts, a sweet and sour hodgepodge of smells rub shoulders. Dream a little... Imagine a slinky, Parisian kept woman slithering lithely out of her parked *austeen mini,* perhaps sporting Hermès' Calèche, the perfume most made to mingle with feline furs and the whiplash elegance of handmade riding boots.

As the lady enters the majestic doorway of her apartment building in the seventh *arrondissement* recently upgraded district, one of those *porte cochères* originally built to accomodate horse-drawn carriages, she is greeted not by a hasty, passionate, *baiser volé* of a kiss from her mature Parisian lover, but rather by the homely aroma of the *concierge's potage* vegetable soup, spiced with herbs from her native Provence.

A *je ne sais quoi*

Such are the subtleties of Parisian nostalgia. Gentle whiffs that hint at the city's much celebrated *je ne sais quoi.* Olfactory traits that meant Maurice Chevalier could sing *Paris je t'aime* from the bottom of his heart, on any stage in the world.

No question about it. There is something special about *this* capital. It is something about the way she looks into her own eyes. So self-assured. So self-satisfied. Watching her own silhouette mirrored in chic store windows as she walks by. Under the arches of the rue de Rivoli. Rue de la Pompe. Rue du Bac. Constantly looking at herself in the mirror. From the Eiffel Tower's crisscross girders. From the Tour Montparnasse's upper floors. From the city's latest monument, Beaubourg museum of modern art, with its bird's eye view escalators gliding through transparent intestine tunnels.

Paris spends hours in the bath narcissistically chasing her own image reflected in the Seine. Taking endless round trips aboard *bateaux mouches,* pleasure boats, for the sheer enjoyment of seeing herself just one more time.

Vanity is Paris' name. Even women tend to see Paris as a woman. Frivolous. Spendthrift. Adorable. Fascinating, but also forbidding. A challenge to their feminity. In no city is it more uncomfortable for a woman to feel drab and penniless. Gifts and clothes are flaunted in shop windows, with taunting, tantalizing refinement. To tempt the customer is a fine art in France. Parisian boutiques have the most wickedly alluring displays in France.

True—even a wreckless creature like Paris has her limits. A project for having most of the skyscrapers "like we in America aren't building them any more" the *super moderne* La Défense precinct designed in fully reflective glass so that the whole of Paris could be seen in it from the avenue de la Grande-Armée was eventually abandoned as too costly an enterprise for "times of austerity" and potentially distracting for the city's drivers who it was thought would do better to keep their eyes on the road.

Paris is an attractive, distracting beauty. A treacherous beauty.

The money-grabbing, hyper-ambitious capital co-exists with the ordinary man's day-to-day Paris. Paris is above all home for over 10 million inhabitants (including the suburbs), 10 million cheeky Parisian sparrows each trying to get a word in, each struggling against unemployment, each striving to build a nest.

Postcard Paris and Paris *by night* do exist, but there is also a more down-to-earth Paris.

Paris is a capital with sublime, ethereal rose-windows in its great churches and modest geranium-clad balconies in its more village-like districts.

A rose by any other name

Paris is a rose is a rose is a rose. Like the socialist rose on the party posters plastered all over the city at election time. A gipsy rose, at heart, in the depths of the *métro*.

Paris is an exquisite rose-window like those of Notre Dame and la Sainte Chapelle. A haughty, solitary rose playing "hide and seek" in the *Jardin du Luxembourg* gardens, shielding teasingly behind a sign that warns *il est interdit de marcher sur la pelouse* (keep off the grass). An artificial, plastic rose, sold on the market, among the toilet requisites, by the picturesque stalls displaying local and exotic fruits, pats of butter and jugs of thick cream, heaps of giant, fresh eggs, muttons' heads, suckling pigs decorated as for a jazz funeral, wriggling shellfish, monster-sized tuna and tiny sardines. Rue Mouffetard. Rue de Seine.

Paris is a shocking pink rosebud intricately embroidered on the black lace trimmings of a naughty brassiere, worn by a transvestite, offering himself in the Bois de Boulogne. Late, late a night.

Paris is a silk rose painstakingly sewn by a *midinette,* slaving milliner's assistant, and worn by an overbearingly sophisticated lady attending the Prix de l'Arc de Triomphe at Longchamp race course.

Paris is a rose. Tossed admiringly at a *danseuse étoile* star ballerina at the Paris Opera. The rose that makes all that disciplined training as a *petit rat* seem worthwhile. Paris is a rose, a single red rose bought after the show from a slender flower-seller dressed in blue jeans and worn-out shetland pullover. Bought for a pretty girl, in long, couturier-designed frock. In a restaurant in the Halles district, where the market used to be before it was transferred to Rungis in 1969. For a pretty Parisienne. Lips gleeming with carefully applied lipstick. Cheeks glowing with rouge. A pretty *Parisienne* who kisses that red rose. In the candlelight. Over a bowl of onion soup. A corny, sentimental red rose. A rose with thorns.

A breath-taking bird's-eye view of the city-scape from a perch 300 meters off the ground where a painter hangs suspended retouching the high-flown iron lattice of the Eiffel Tower — the first disruption of the Paris skyline in 1889 (preceding page).   Today's controversy and criticism has shifted focus from the Eiffel Tower, now the city's most visited landmark, to the 56 storey Montparnasse Tower's puncturing a once harmonious perspective dominated by the dome of the Panthéon.   Past and present are again telescoped into focus juxtaposing the medieval

cathedral of Notre Dame and the Pompidou art
center, Centre Beaubourg, inaugurated in
January 77 to heated pro-and con-troversy.
Thus the city tries to reconcile the old and the new.
Below: Downstream from the Ile Saint Louis,
the Ile de la Cité where it all began — Paris
spiralling outward from a primitive island
settlement to spread over both sides of the Seine.
Following page: the tower blocks of La
Défense, the biggest high-rise project of the de
Gaulle-Pompidou era, dominate
the view West over Paris.

Oases of open space inviting promenades, contemplation and escape from the city's hustle and bustle. Gardens galore of formal floral patterns groomed to geometrical perfection. The Tuileries Gardens, already a fashionable meeting place for Parisians in the early 17th century, provide an ideal vantage point to capture the odd resonance between Napoleon's two triumphal arches, the Arc de Triomphe du Carrousel and its bigger counterpart crowning the majestic sweep of the Champs-Elysées. Rising up between the Arcs is the famed Egyptian obelisk erected in dead center of the Place de la Concorde, site of the guillotine throughout the Reign of Terror — rolling the heads of Louis XVI, Marie Antoinette, Madame du Barry, Charlotte Corday... gruesome memories far from the giddy thoughts of camera-clicking tourists (following page).

Parisian pot-pourri of history and folklore, a patchwork of traditions. On horseback a Republican Guard dreams of Carolingian knights in shining armor. On the job firemen in their burnished helmets, the ubiquitous newspaper vendor in his kiosk, a first class Metro traveller careful of the company he keeps, flag-toting war veterans, and to many the very symbol of Paris itself, the chic Parisienne striding out on Avenue George V, seemingly oblivious to the policing she's getting. Such are the contrasts of the daily Paris scene.

Even today the Place de la Bastille holds its place in revolutionary mythology and is a symbolic port of call for most left-wing demonstrations and processions. A rainbow-splash of banners are assembled for the May Day parade under the watchful figure of the Spirit of Liberty atop the 150-foot July column commemorating those who died during the revolts of 1830 and 1848.

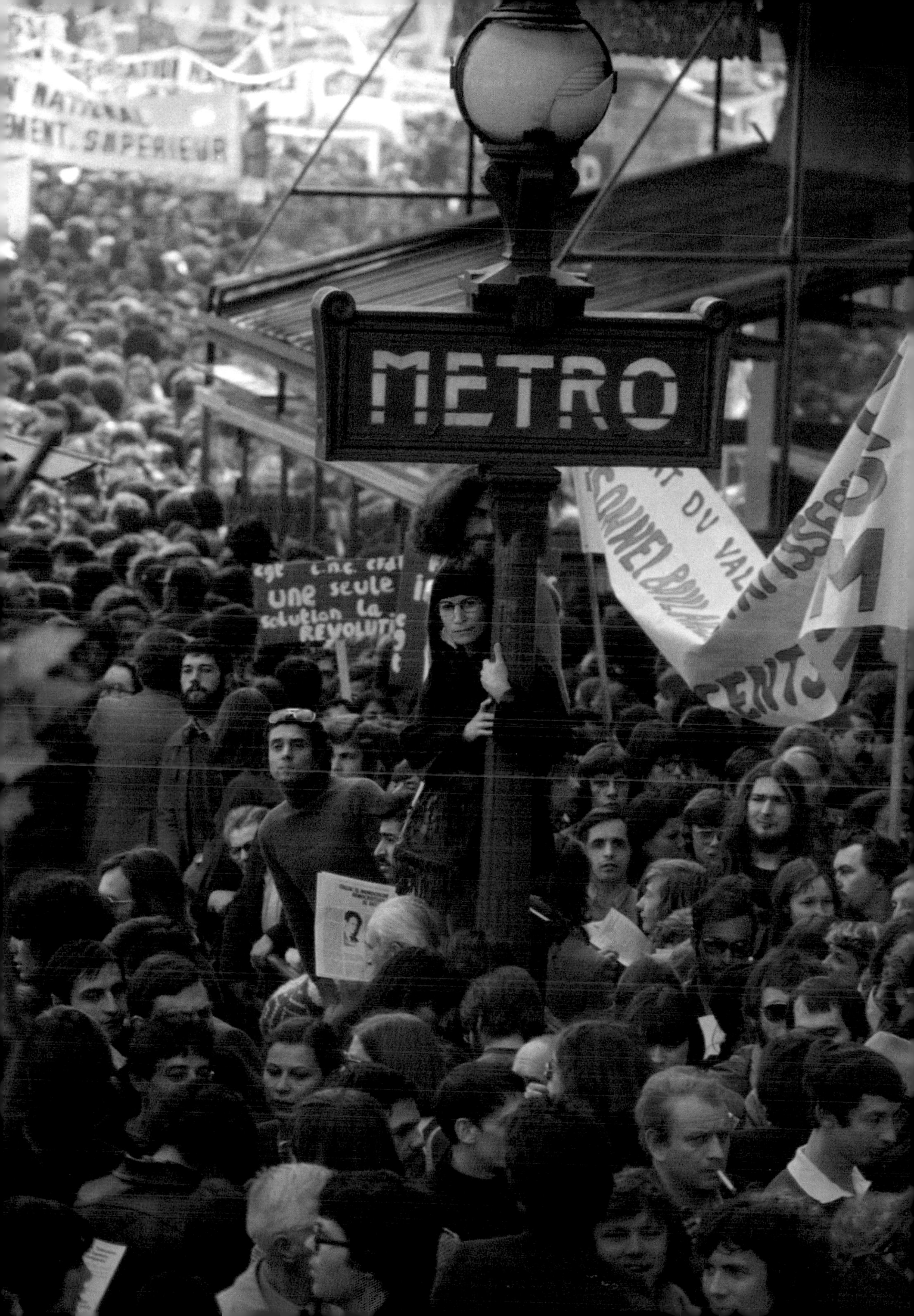
METRO
une seule
solution la

Noblesse oblige

No matter where one looks in Paris, outward manifestations abound bearing witness to the existence of a past rich in importance, splendor, and tradition. Nonetheless, as in every great world capital, it is best not to look too far behind the great facades and edifices to examine the foundations on which the "grandeur" of that past is built. Paris is a place of outlandish contradictions, ambiguities, and fascinating illusions.

Take the countless monuments to France's military past to those who died in battle. Depending upon ones point of view, there is either something sacred and exalted or else something dangerously unhealthy, tragically wasteful, and basically ridiculous about such glorification of mass slaughter.

Verdun is a prime example of the manner in which ambiguous battles become great victories through an odd emotional and mental process, evidently based on the amount of French blood shed. At Verdun, half of the 2,000,000 men sent to battle were killed. The situation reached such extremity that the French regulars launched a strike, for which many more were shot by their own government. At Verdun, the ruthless division of classes which plagues French society became blood-curdlingly obvious as the élite "sacrificed" the "lower" classes—the infantry—to German cannons. Today, however, that battle is well-remembered as a major French victory, part of the French military's grand tradition.

Even those French who have little use either for France's military past or its present Army are somewhat moved by the annual parade down the Champs-Elysées of armed men and weapons on the 14th of July. This seeming paradox, is traditional. Remember, after all, that Stendhal's Julien Sorel renounced the Army but never threw away the locket that contained a hidden portrait of Napoleon.

While July 14th has been largely confiscated for peripatetic demonstrations of France's "*force de frappe*" strike force, a much more humanistic Parisian tradition—*les petits bals de quartier* which gather entire neighborhoods together to eat, drink, talk, dance has begun to disappear. In the working class neighborhoods of the 18th, 19th, and 20th arrondissements, where *les bals* still exist, young folk are often to be found shaking to the latest American or English rock group while their parents and grandparents sit on the sidelines sipping another *petit blanc,* talking to one another in soft tones about earlier *bals* and regretting the demise of the *java* dance fashionable in their day.

In his search for a *métier,* Julien Sorel's alternative to Army red was Church black. In this, too, Paris has changed. The city boasts hundreds of churches, from the Gothic splendor of Notre-Dame de Paris to the dime-store tinsel of the *Sacré-Cœur,* with numerous neighborhood churches like *Notre-Dame-de-Lorette, Trinité* and *St-Philippe-du-Roule* in between. Yet the Roman Catholic tradition's part in the population's daily life has become minimal. Anti-clerical humor, once a main-stay of French thought, has all but disappeared from French political and satirical magazines, a sure sign that the Church is no longer considered a dangerous enemy by anyone.

Central to everything that happens in France, Paris is the center of the French language. People tend to be judged by the ease and precision (or lack of same) with which they speak.

Adamant in claiming that theirs is the language of the truly civilized and cultured, the French are defensive about the steady encroachment of the American language into the domains of international business and diplomacy. Such defense of the language is also traditional. It is presided over by the 40 "Immortals" under the Coupole of the Académie Française. Founded as a gentlemen's club, and shortly afterwards declared the official guardian of the language by Richelieu and Louis XIV in 1635, the Académie Française retains the spirit of an élitist club. Its forty members are elected from the nobility, old families, the military and other professions, with the remainder made up of writers and artists. No woman has ever been named an Immortal; neither were Balzac, Stendhal, Flaubert, Zola, Proust, Gide, Sartre, Camus, nor Baudelaire. The Académie carries out two functions: endless editing of a comprehensive multi-volume dictionary, and passing judgement on every word spoken by their countrymen. "Franglais" is so much the bane of the Académie that a law was recently pushed through making it illegal to use foreign (again especially American) words in public advertising and official communications. Most Parisians speak of "le weekend" in ordinary conversation, yet, they may no longer take weekend charter flights, but must book seats on a *"vol nolisé"* or *"vol affrété"*. The Académie is so slow to act that travel agents will talk to a customer about the savings involved in a *"vol charter"* while filling out an official form for a *"vol nolisé"*.

Concern with ones personal appearance (apparel in particular) began as a ploy by Louis XIV to maintain economic and social control over his court. Still, both fashion and *savoir faire* which tells you what to do with it, come naturally to Parisians. It has to do with the French view of reality and nature. To the French, nature is there to be controlled, shaped into an ideal. The young Parisian's narrowly cut, precisely pressed jeans worn with exactly the right shirt "casually" tucked into his belt and open to mid-chest, is but one more expression of that sensibility which insists that gardens be laid out according to carefully balanced designs, with trees and shrubs that conform to an imposed pattern.

To appreciate the full force of Parisian elegance, one should attend a *soirée de gala* at the Opéra, when the grand staircase fulfills its original functions becoming a grand and sweeping stage for gowns, jewels, furs, *smokings* (dinner jackets), and, above all, class, paraded with seemingly unconscious grace. After a change of costume the same women and men can be seen at fashionable restaurants or night-clubs, or at the races at Longchamp, Chantilly, and Deauville. Fashion and elegance are everywhere. It is hardly an accident that the average Parisian spends more for boots, a skirt, or "the perfect coat" than for rent or food.

Well, perhaps not for more than for food.

If there is any tradition in France based as firmly on the present as on the past, its foundation is the Parisian dining table. The Parisian is obsessed with food and its preparation. Common conversation often consists of discussing meals one has eaten or which one is planning to eat, such discussions taking place indeed even as one is eating.

Eating *en famille* in the Auvergne in the middle of France, I sat across from a charming ancient lady who had returned, to the family farm after many years in Paris. When I admitted to being an American, she smiled sadly and said "Ah yes, America. It seems they do not eat well there. My brother once visited America, and they served him *rôti* and *fromage* on the same plate!"

The most important tradition in Paris is the grandeur of Paris itself. Parisians, and all Frenchmen, believe that no city can compare with her, that if something is Parisian it is by definition both elegant and properly aligned with the order of the universe. As one strolls along the Seine in the magic evening light, it is easy to agree with them. However, that "tradition" which has it that all things Parisian are above reproach is disturbing. An ex-*concierge* of mine once chastised me about American racism. I admitted it existed, hoped that things were improving and went on to note that she herself could hardly be a stranger to racism since it existed in France as well. "But, Monsieur, surely that isn't true. You know very well yourself that Paris is famous for its lack of racism." Ah, I said, then I had misunderstood the Parisian attitude towards the Arabs and other immigrant workers. "Ah, the Arabs! Now we are speaking of an inferior race, Monsieur!" No amount of talking could convince her that her attitude might be described as racist, for "Everyone knows there is no racism in Paris." It is traditional.

It is also traditional, and part of the city's greatness, that just as you have had enough of Paris, and have begun to think of her more as bitch than as an elegant lady, she slips up behind you in the grey light of dawn to whisper softly and kiss you on the ear, and you fall in love with her all over again.

July 14 commemorates the capture of the state prison, the Bastille, by the people of Paris in 1789, hailed as a great victory for the Revolution despite the fact only 7 prisoners were in the fortress at the time. The symbol of the King's arbitrary power was subsequently demolished and a fête nationale celebrated every year by a military parade marching down the mile-long Champs-Elysées. Filing past in step with the rigors of pomp and circumstance are the cadets of the Saint-Cyr military academy, scores of Garde Republicain cavalrymen, an endless swirl of marines, generals galore in the official tribune and foursomes of students from the Grandes Ecoles. Lots of flash and splash in a grandiose setting that never ceases to rouse national fervor.

Napoleon left Paris with the largest triumphal arch in the world, yet he never lived to see it completed: his remains were carried beneath the great arch on December 15, 1840 on the way to their final resting place in the Invalides. The victory parade of WWI allied troops was held here on July 14, 1919, and the following year the body of an unknown soldier was buried beneath the arch marked by an eternal flame. It was also here that de Gaulle proclaimed the Liberation of Paris on August 26, 1944.

A Republican Guard stands ready to defend l'Elysée, the Presidential palace. The Senate holds forth in the Luxembourg palace built in the early 17th century, while the Palais Bourbon, known today as the Assemblée Nationale, houses the seat of Deputies constituting the lower house of the French legislature. At the Palais de Justice (right) the judiciary keeps a solemn eye on the executive and legislative branches of the French government.

More Republican Guards. This time not to honor military or political power but intellectual supremacy — or so one is to believe. On the banks of the Seine opposite the Louvre stands the palace of the Institut de France made up of five academies of learning, most famous of which is the Académie Française (created by Richelieu in 1635) followed by Les Inscriptions et Belles Lettres (1663), Les Sciences (1666), Les Beaux-Arts (1795), Les Sciences Morales et Politiques (1832). New members of the Académie Française decked out in the traditional green-embroidered uniform designed in 1795 are received beneath the glorious dome where they make a speech in praise of their predecessor, while their own career is glowingly described by another Academician. As impressive as those admitted have been those bypassed: Descartes, Pascal, Molière, Diderot, Balzac, Maupassant, Proust, Zola... Following page: Many great moments in French history have been celebrated in Notre Dame under the kaleidoscopic brilliance of the stained glass windows. From the coronation of Napoleon as Emperor on December 2, 1804 to the continuing ordination of priests, magnificence has been the hallmark of this awesome 13th century cathedral, the very symbol of Paris.

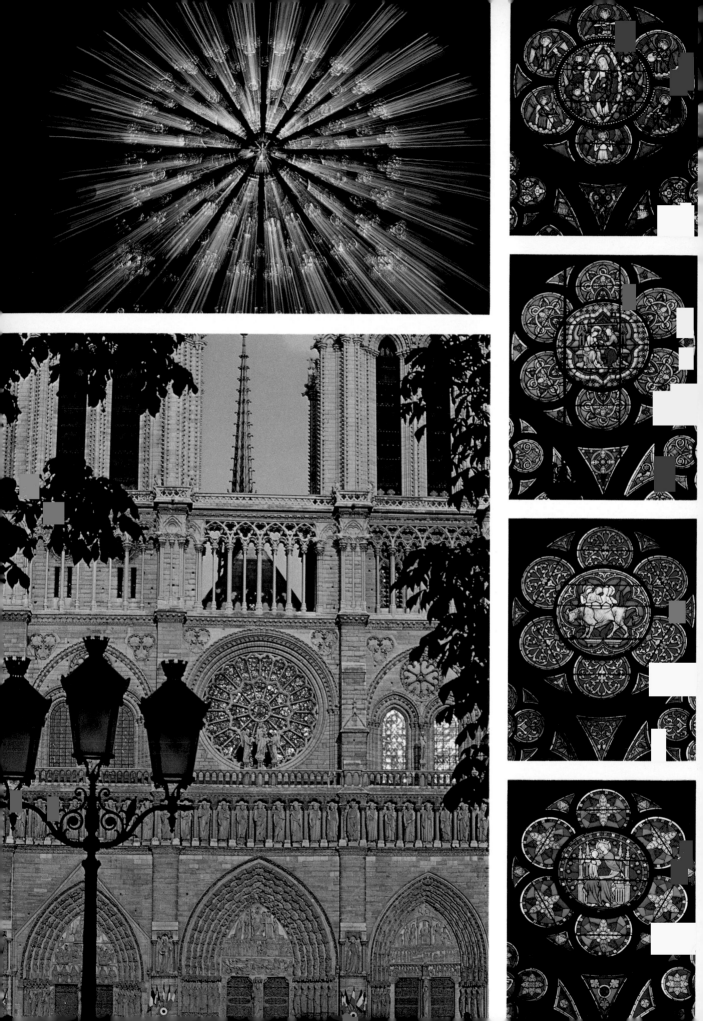

Work on the Paris Opera began
in 1862, but by the time it was
finished the Second Empire had
fallen, victim of the Franco-
Prussian War.   Even though
inaugurated in 1875 under the
Third Republic, the Opera
remains a dazzling architectural
reflection of the glittering,
materialistic society of the
France of Napoleon III. (It took
architect Charles Garnier no
less than 33 kilometers of
blueprints to design!) Today,
production and maintenance
costs are a matter of grave
concern despite a government
subsidy, and it is only on Gala
evenings that Garnier's
materpiece, the great staircase,
appears in its true glory, lined
with Republican Guards whose
uniforms hark back to the
Second Empire.   So much a
part of the scene is the great
staircase, it is even evoked in the
décor of an Opera Ballet
production, outdoors in the
Louvre's Cour Carrée.

*Maxim's, one of the city's most famous
restaurants founded in 1893 owes as much to its
faithfully preserved 1900 décor and its beau
monde clientele as it does to the
world-famous quality of its food.
In spite of Coco Chanel's death in 1971 her
fashion house lives on with ever elegant Chanel
models still descending the famous flattering
staircase (previous double page). Paris and the
haute couture are almost synonymous — with
fashion, luxury, elegance and style the
keynotes of this city more than any other.*

So seriously does Paris take the art of gastronomy that admired chefs like Raymond Oliver of the Grand Véfour (1799) enjoy the kind of star status usually reserved elsewhere for successful writers, actors, and artists. True to the fervor the art demands, cavistes *in the wine celler of Maxim's lunch among the grand* crus *they watch over. At the Tour d'Argent a pinch of herbs is added to a sauce with the finesse that elevates cooking to gastronomic art. In the kitchen of Maxim's a chef approaches his* langoustines *with the respect of a painter approaching his canvas.*

The annual Grand Prix at the Longchamps racetrack is a favourite gathering place for « Le Tout Paris » (the city's fashionable set) who effortlessly project Parisian chic

Le chic *is a very Parisian thing and it is cultivated like a hot-house plant. Select enclaves of* chic *are nestled away in the Bois de Boulogne catering to those in the know (and in the money):a perfumed walk among prize-winning roses at Bagatelle, luncheon outdoors on the terrace of La Grande Cascade (once the hunting lodge of Napoleon III), a game of polo at the exclusive Polo Club... A lazy afternoon aperitif on Fouquet's Champs-Elysées terrace is undeniably* chic... *as is (following pages) a trot on horseback in the lacey shadows of the Eiffel Tower.*

View from Beaubourg

Even Beaubourg's firmest detractors have to admire the view from Georges Pompidou Cultural Center's 5th floor terrace. At helicopter height, the eye uncovers historic Paris. We glide over the Tour St. Jacques, survey the spires of Saint Louis' Sainte Chapelle, scan the Panthéon and Invalides domes, and bump smack into the Tour Montparnasse. From this distance, and at dusk, the jolt is muted. Now, look back on Beaubourg from Montparnasse—what's that flat, unfinished factory doing there?

Towers and gigantic cultural centers are meant to be seen from, not gazed upon. The Eiffel Tower, too, was once called an atrocity. Beaubourg will become in time another jolly giant.

At first, public imagination balked at the $200 million cultural King Kong, a top-heavy investment in a country whose provincial museums starve for funds. In the immediate neighborhood, resentment ran high. The 11th century village, Beau Bourg, had been a highly respectable place to live: Pascal was born there, and foreign bankers, such as Scot, John Law and Swiss, Jacques Necker with his daughter, Madame de Staël, flourished. Then, came the Revolution. Prostitutes and thieves, always lurking nearby, came out of hiding and took over. Beaubourg became highly disreputable, noted for its low life. The Center has opened up the throbbing main artery, the original east-west axis where Lutetia's Roman roads were traced. It has pumped life into the heart of the old city.

Paris is a palimpsest—nothing is buried forever. Not even beheaded kings. Revolutionaries went so far as to decapitate the great sculpted Kings of Judea from Notre-Dame Cathedral. Sold for scrap, they were bought up by a royalist who immured them in the walls of a present-day bank near the Opéra, the Banque Française du Commerce Extérieur. There, during recent modernization efforts, they were discovered and put on display, in good company, with the prized Lady and Unicorn tapestry at the Cluny Museum. So with Beaubourg, the spearhead of mass culture. Treasures that belonged only to kings are accessible to the public on a grand scale: goodies and gadgets in an enticing automat.

Richard Rodgers, co-architect with Renzo Piano, of the six-storey steel-and-glass edifice, describes it as a building "turned inside-out". All the utilities traditionally concealed are flaunted as decorative elements—hot-water pipes painted in aggressive colors, the snaky umbilical cord of an escalator, conveying visitors to the top-floor Museum of Modern Art, where shows like "Paris-New York" draw capacity crowds. The Public Information Library is a hit: France's first major open-stack library, it offers a tempting array of documentary material including audio-visual language courses. Underground, in Pierre Boulez' Acoustical-Musical Research Institute (IRCAM), experimental masters such as Xenakis, Berio and Stockhausen have a high time coordinating technology and contemporary music.

Eastward from Beaubourg lies the once aristocratic Marais where the Festival du Marais and Festival Estival reign all summer long. There is chamber music at Hôtel de Sully: the Duc de Sully, Henri IV's Minister, allowed his wife as many lovers as she wished, provided they didn't clutter up his stairway; Kipling's Jungle Book in mime and masks on the lucious green lawn of Hôtel de Marle; and an all-women brass band at delightful Marché Sainte-Catherine square.

These days, everybody hangs out on the Duc de Sully's staircase. Students dance the streets and smoke on the stoops of Hôtel des Ambassadeurs de Hollande, where Beaumarchais wrote "The Marriage of Figaro". There is late jazz on the Ile Saint-Louis and even later dining outdoors, among the linden trees below 15th century St-Gervais church. Illuminated at night, the Marais could be another country, another epoch. We step back in time, listening to horses' hoofs on the cobblestones as the last postal wagon comes home to roost in the Café de la Gare's courtyard.

Just as Molière's *troupe* was an itinerant enterprise, moving from the Marais to the left bank and back again, before settling down to inhabit the Comédie Française, so the new *café-théâtre* fringe theater is being tugged toward the Marais. The famed Café de la Gare is just one example. It started up in the sixties near Montparnasse maintime station with young talent: Romain Bouteille, Coluche, Gérard Depardieu, Miou-Miou. When the area around the Gare was torn down to build the Tower, the *troupe* moved to rue du Temple, the street that cuts a fine line between the Marais and Beaubourg.

Does this thronging to Paris' oldest section mean that the rest of the city is a cultural desert? Hardly. Unlike New York or London, Paris never had a real theater district. There are the *grands boulevards,* garish streets leading from the Opéra to the old city gate of St-Denis. But the boulevards, as everybody knows, produce mainly Boulevard comedies, those bedroom farces creaking with stale jokes on cuckoldry.

The avant-garde has definitely gone east with the Théâtre de l'Est Parisien, big on Brecht and, above all, Ariane Mnouchkine and her disciples freaking out at the extraordinary Cartoucherie de Vincennes. Since Mnouchkine took over the old armory with her pageants on French revolution, remote Vincennes has become a new center. Peter Brook set up shop to the north, first with the "Ik", then with "Ubu" in the drafty, magical *Bouffes du Nord.*

While Laurent Terzieff, the man who brought Edward Albee and Murray Schisgal to France, is doing his thing at Lucernaire Forum, an abandoned sawmill off Montparnasse.

Paris is a movie feast: one can see more films from more contries than in any other capital—first-run hits in the center of town, revivals in unexpected haunts, such as the 14th arrondissement's Olympic Entrepôt which is, *naturellement,* a converted warehouse. Where these days, does a theater look like a theater and not a banana warehouse? Well, there's always the Comédie Française.

There are other havens: the Rodin Museum and sculpture garden off stately rue de Varenne. The Russian Conservatory, quai de New-York, where thick borscht is served in the basement to thick accents and wild, tragi-comic violin strains rain from above. The Paris Opéra remains beautifully straight-faced and forbidding; here goes a fresh generation of diligent *petits rats,* with their eternally watchful mothers.

Between those two poles of innovation—the Tour Montparnasse on the left bank, Beaubourg on the right, much uprooting has gone on.

Saint-Germain-des-Prés galleries have opened annexes near Beaubourg: their owners know which way the wind is blowing. So? What artist would not want to get into Beaubourg?

Meanwhile, the students, the children of May '68 ride high on mo-peds, share maids' rooms, scrounge for jobs and sit it out in cafés, discussing ways of making a better society. They still play music on the Pont Neuf, sing in subway stations, shout slogans at demonstrations, buy tacky clothes at the Flea Market, lounge in the Luxembourg Gardens and nuzzle under the bridges of the Seine, wherever Pompidou's expressway leaves some margin for lovers. Although they don't look it, they are trying to hack out a coherent place for themselves within a system they decry. And they are hanging on to their joy. Forever on the fringe, driven from their beloved left bank, they seek new stamping grounds.

The drift today is towards Beaubourg, the epitome of popular culture. On the plaza in front of the Center, jugglers and fire eaters do their tricks. So do the neighborhood dogs, taking full advantage of Paris' first major pedestrian zone. Students munch on *crêpes* from the local *crêperie,* a stone's throw from rue St-Denis where the "girls" wield the whips of their century-old specialty trade.

So much has changed in this city. Ancient Paris has been knocked, poked, drilled and scraped. Yet, come the revolution, or not, the bread is the best, and the circuses aren't bad either. No doubt about it, the lady is still lovely.

A royal palace in the 16th and 17th centuries, the Louvre did not become a museum until the Revolution. First opened to the public on August 10, 1793 it wasn't until 1965 that André Malraux, France's then Minister of Culture, arranged for several bronze statues by sculptor Aristide Maillol to be set on to the lawns of the Palace du Carrousel. With the state-seized royal collection providing the museum's nucleus, art from all over the world has come to make the Louvre one of the most fabulous treasure-troves of all time — offering a comprehensive record of the achievements of Western civilization and of the civilizations which influenced its development. Star attractions from Egyptian sarcophigi to the Venus de Milo have been immortalized the world over.

It is no mystery that the
performing arts are inextricably
bound to dicipline.   The
rigorous school of dance at the
Opera is a training ground for
the stars of tomorrow known
today simply as « petits rats »
or little mice.   Was it this star-
dust hankering unleashed in
these child/women that
Degas (lower left)
wished to capture?

Paris has not forgotten the open-air origins of theatre, music and dance, and as soon as the bad weather lifts, summer Festivals use the city's historic monuments as a backdrop for an explosion of talent in the performing arts.   While classical music resounds in the courtyard of a glorious hôtel particulier in the Marais or in the Roman ruins of the Cluny Museum, street theatre animates Saint-Germain-des-Prés, casting a medieval mood. Throughout the year Paris churches lend their impressive pious settings to a wide range of musical expression.   Most sublime by far is the Ile de la Cité's 13th century royal chapel, Sainte Chapelle (following double page), a shimmering marvel of stained glass and multi-tinted light.

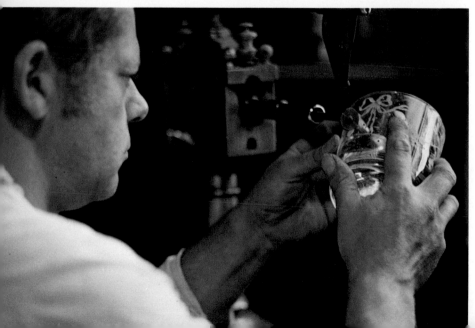

In the back streets of Paris a
die-hard breed of craftsmen still
practice skills handed down
through generations... In the
Marais a stringed-instrument
maker, a glass engraver working
for Christian Dior, an ivory
sculptor on the rue Bonaparte...
artisans at the service of music,
fashion, and sculpture.

THE VISITORS ARE REMINDED
THAT IT IS STRICTLY PROHIBITED
TO TOUCH THE STATUES

There is some indefinable magic at work in Paris that spurs creativity — sending amateur painters into the streets while inducing students to develop talent in art schools like Montparnasse's Académie de la Grande-Chaumière, leaving others looking at Rodin for inspiration.

What with ever rising rents and the call to modernization doing away with many artists' ateliers there is no one artists' quarter like the hey-days of Montmartre and Montparnasse. The official residence of twentieth-century art in Paris is, of course, the Centre Beaubourg, a break with tradition in more ways than meet the eye (following page).

Saint-Germain-des-Prés and the cafés that played a pivotal rôle in fostering intellectual and artistic life before and after WW II, notably the Café de Flore (favourite haunt of Sartre, Simone de Beauvoir and Genet), the Deux-Magots (host to self-proclaimed founder of surrealism André Breton), and across the boulevard the Brasserie Lipp (where social careers have been ended over night by a turn-down from iron-willed proprietor Roger Cazes). Needless to say intellectuals and tourists alike still cluster on these illustrious terraces to watch the world go by, though Sartre is nowhere to be seen. Down towards the river on the rue de Seine, the picturesque café-bar La Palette (opposite) attracts a young student couple.

The Panthéon (top left), burial ground of great men from Victor Hugo to Resistance hero Jean Moulin; the amphitheatres of the Sorbonne university (bottom left); the Luxembourg Gardens (right) offering a haven for students in pursuit of reading, or of each other.   These are the things the university quarter are made of.

Impassioned students. What would Paris be without them? Ever since May '68 student activist movements have gained momentum, becoming a very real political force with the voting age now lowered to 18. Whether marching for the cause of immigrant workers or contesting the tactics of the state's CRS stormtrooping brigades, leftist students in the true Paris tradition take to the streets for better or for worse.

The scenes are familiar ones to Parisians: provocative political posters by students at the Beaux-Arts... demonstrations, banners, helmets in hand in anticipation of police brutality. A city wrenched by conflicts, battered by beliefs... teargas and tears, a far cry from the innocent joviality of the annual Beaux-Arts school ball (following page).

Selfportrait with neighbors

Parisians' Paris is Paris awakening. In a mist of sleep dust. Paris barely able to keep her eyes open, but making a desperate effort. Geraniums swaying in their window boxes. Disturbed in their slumber by a brisk, energetic: "good morning my little flowers. How are you? It's time to get up." In keeping with Parisian ecological awareness. With the belief that plants understand us. That they have feelings like any human being or pet dog. That they can perceive our moods and attitude towards them through our tone of voice alone. "Now I'm going to have to move you. Coffee smells good, doesn't it? I always add a couple of spoonfuls of chicory."

(Exit Geraniums). Enter a heap of bed linen. Paris in the morning is tag day everyday. With sheets, blankets, pillows and bolsters hauled out to be shaken one by one in the crisp, dawn air. Moist and warm as freshly baked bread. Bedding left to hang, like flags, still limp, exhausted by their occupant's tossing and turning, a prey to metropolitan anxiety dreams. Will the *patron,* boss, have been suitably impressed by the "*en famille,* something quite simple" dinner that practically broke the family budget yesterday evening?

Behind Paris' shutters, Parisian minds boggle in face of such unknowns. Hard-pressed wives are harrassed with questions: "but, you know *mon chou,* my cabbage, that you are my *conseillère,* my advisor. Just think. Where would I be without you? Now, tell me will I be promoted? Will Dupont's *piston* (pressure) and recommandation, serve us? Did you send him our best wishes for the New Year?" (silence, total silence). "Are you listening to me? I tell you, you never listen to me. You don't understand. You refuse to understand. Where's that going to get us? You are no use..." (silence, total silence). Then, suddenly the reaction comes: a shrill, chilling shrewish sound, an *oooaaarrrhhh* like the scream of a Parisian lover throwing himself from the top of the Eiffel tower. Brought to a screeching halt by an embarrassed, but firm: "Les voisins!"

In Paris, "les voisins" (the neighbors) are crucial. Parisians are *blasé* about everything in Paris. Everything but "les voisins".

In Paris, a Scottish highlander in full regional dress complete with sporran and silk ribboned cap, making his way up the rue de Rivoli toward the Louvre for "a wee look at the Mona Lisa" would not get so much as a glance from the average Parisian. Sure. He would be thought "ridiculous" on sight, but Parisians pretend to mind their own business. They stare. They glare. Yet, they would never turn round to watch that Scot continue on his way. That would be to show interest. To pay unwarranted attention to a *m'as-tu vu?* (did you notice me?) type and Parisians never, never take any notice of anyone, except for "les voisins". Their neighbors. With whom they have a love-hate relationship, for they are "obliged to take them into account."

Rushed breakfasts can be bad mood conducive anywhere, and in Paris affect driving as well as behavior in the *métro*. Parisian secretaries often gulp gruellingly short coffee and dry croissant breakfasts standing-up in a dismal café opposite their *bureau* (office). Standing uneasily on a carpet of waste paper and crushed cigarette ends which have not yet been cleared. Parisians' Paris can be as decadent as slick Paris is refined.

Hard-pressed Madame X (seen above) may begin her day by having words with a character who counts as much as "les voisins", by extension: the *concierge*. In a Parisian apartment building the *concierge* can make or break a tenant's reputation with his neighbors. And that is crucial. So, the *concierge's* palm is usually as well greased as the roasts she cooks in her oven, imbuing the whole staircase with before-and-after cooking smells. The Parisian *concierge* is untouchable. A sacred cow. She has power and she exercises it. Slouching around imperiously in overall, and slippers. With clips and *bigoudis* (rollers) in her hair. "No, Madame X. I cannot tell you if you have any more mail this morning. I haven't had the time to sort it all yet. You should know that. Just think. Where would I be if I gave all my tenants a preview?"

Madame X pursues her helter-skelter rush to work, accompanying her children to school. Parisians' schedules are tight, tight, tight.

Madame X stops by at the baker's: "Quick—Monsieur— A *petit pain au chocolat* (chocolate bun) for my younger one's *goûter* (afternoon snack)". Advantage to the baker. Power: "Just think Madame, we've been up since six this morning. You want to rise earlier. The world belongs to those who get up early!"

Such is Parisians' Paris, in the morning. The working day continues with more tenterhooks, for the French *patron* (boss), is far from easy-going. He is aware of his responsibility for seeing to it that his employees are productive and operational. Constantly. If French employees are notorious for trying to cheat the *patron* and the system he represents, for preferring to be *souffrant* (sick) than "on vacation", it is perhaps a question of balance of power. Parisians consider that it is better to cheat than to be cheated. That is their idea of integrity. *Par exemple* (for example), lunch hours in Paris are for eating in. *Vu?* (Got it?). If you have something else to do during lunch-time, you have lunch first and then do it. It's your right to do so. Even if you do quiver and quake at the prospect of the *patron's* reaction.

While the Parisian *métro* (subway) is the place where Parisian class distinction is most flagrant, in Paris, bistros at lunch-time are neutral class territory. Boss and employees share eating haunts. So much so that if you have a secret to discuss, it is wise to change district. In *bistros,* walls have ears, *patron's* ears, as sharp as their reprimands. In *bistros,* secretaries and management daily eat a standard meal. At different tables, but in the same setting. Something like... eggs mayonnaise, greasy grilled steak and French fries, camembert or fruit, a quarter bottle of red wine or of mineral water. At the same standard price. Only your yes/no answer to "un café?", brusque equivalent of "and coffee to follow, Sir?", separates the men from the boys, as does possession of a home-based wife or "concubine" (which is an administrative status in France) on whom to get you own back for the traffic warden's parking fine, or for the *patron's* momentous "Would you mind coming into my *bureau* for a moment? Shut the door, please. No. I'm afraid I will come straight to the point, I cannot give you an increase. However, I must make it clear to you that your position here, with us, does have a future. Show initiative. Keep in line. And you will soon see that you get places in this firm."

Emmerdant! The word and its whole excremental family has just been adopted officially by the Académie Française's "Immortals". Enough to make founder Richelieu turn and shiver in his grave.

"Now that's really *emmerdant! mon chou,* my little cabbage." Tinker or tailor, Parisians are equal before their *patrons.* They have to watch brain-numbing T.V. programs when they get back home, beyond the *concierge's* enquiring eagle eye, just so they can forget the *patron.*

So much for ordinary, day-to-day, lived-in Parisian's Paris. But there is an alternative, crazier, zanier kind of Parisian. Sometimes he turns out to be the same Parisian, in disguise. In cloak and dagger. Freaky. Punky. The *Tout Paris* adict. Just as the tough but classy whores, who parade nonchalantly in the *contre-allée* sidewalk of wooded, wealthy Avenue Foch at nightime can be seen window shopping in the afternoon on Faubourg Saint Honoré like any other lady of means, in prim, irreprochable *ensembles* two piece suits, so some Parisians, lead a double life.

The shop assistant who cuts down on meals to keep slim and to save for a couture punk outfit in black chamois and midnight-blue pure silk (tatters and lamé razor blades, chains and rips that cost the earth, for a top Parisian signature) just so that her caddish *fils à papa,* kept-by-daddy, boyfriend won't be ashamed to take her to night spots like Elysée-Matignon, Castel, Régine's, Paradis Latin, Main Bleue... she would not be seen dead in *La Jet Société* now *Punky Paris* is "in", inspired by Punk, the British youth social anger phenomenon taken over by the "Tout Paris", the eternal, super-select "entire Paris crowd". Paris is the city of transcience and tradition, fashion and convention. Parisians' Paris is all things to all Parisians.

Glimpses that make up a city's originality: the rue Saint-Antoine market street with gaily colored awnings, a pedestrian taking his life in hand facing Gallic temperament behind the wheel; the distinctive blue and green street emblem evokes folkloric images ("street of the bad boys"); a policeman on the beat calling for help; the sewer cleaner like Picasso's dove enjoying a noonday flight to freedom. While the pissotières *(last vestiges of male privilege) disappear day by day, the automobile continues to throttle the natural flow of city life.*

4ᵐᵉ ARRᵗ

RUE DES MAUVAIS GARÇONS

What is Paris if not its bistros? *... despite the Russian origin of the word. Bistro! bistro! (quick, quick) shouted Czar Alexander's cossaks on the Champs-Elysées in 1815, clamoring for a drink. Ever since, le bistro has had its special place in Parisians' habits: a lazy respite and refuge from the humdrum of city life, a place to meet and foregather between workday chores, a port of call to rest, refresh and drown ones solitude.*

*Paris-village: despite the invasion of the
combustion engine and grandiose masterplans
for urban renewal, village life has survived in the
middle of a thriving city.   Fresh field flowers
decorate the cobbled street, old friends settle
down to an afternoon aperitif and game of cards,
to the familiar tunes of a street corner
accordionist.*

Fresh fruit and vegetable stands bring the country to the city. The Mouffetard Market (top left), so varied, crowded and colorful makes up a miniature world of its own, offering a daily ritual of local animation most Parisians wouldn't think of missing. It goes without saying a trip to the market wouldn't be complete without a "pause bistrot" *providing a moment of exchange and complicity between housewives on their round of chores. Opposite: The famous L'Escargot restaurant stands in the midst of Montorgueil Market.*

The belly of Paris is always empty, ravenous, carnivorous, clamoring for a daily diet of "biftèque frites". Yet the beef in question may well be a juicy cut of horsemeat from the nearest blood-red chevaline *butcher shop.*

ROUX

CHEVALINE

FRANÇAISE ET VIENNOISE

INTERDIT
DU 16 A FIN DU MOIS

16·31

AU BON PAIN D'AUTREFOIS
Spécialité de PAINS
de CAMPAGNE & de SEIGLE
AU LEVAIN

GERVAIS

Previous page: "Give us our daily bread" could well be the personal prayer of each Parisian for whom it is the most basic of staples, without which a meal can simply not begin. Indeed, the French art of gastronomy begins with the quality of French bread. Top left: the baker's young apprentice earns her living (gagne son pain) by transporting baguettes in the traditional basket to local restaurateurs. Bottom left: When Paris isn't eating meat it turns to tripe — the intestines, the stomach, the liver, any animal organ in fact that isn't exactly meat yet considered edible (though everyone would not agree). Opposite: A typical street encounter between neighboring concierges comparing notes while a solitary gilded horse listens to the murmurs of the city.

*Arches and doorways delimiting space,
separating "quartiers", creating perspectives,
forming passageways, framing views of secret
gardens and multitudes alike.
Below: the Porte Saint-Denis,
with its endless stream of traffic.*

Strangers in a strange land. At the foot of Montmartre's alabaster-white basilica of the Sacré-Cœur lies the quartier known as the "Goutte d'Or", the African slum area of Paris. The meter-maid (bottom left) is from the Antilles. Opposite: An arab in traditional dress coming from the Left Bank Mosque stops to get his bearings in a town where the welcome is not always warm.

In spite of overwhelming odds, the expanding
network of supermarkets has not swallowed up
the traditional "petits commerçants". Even the
most unusual tastes can be satisfied by the city's
labyrinth of speciality shops and regional
boutiques providing products often unavailable
on the mass market. Regional tastes and habits
flourish in this urban microcosm of France...
uprooted Bretons (opposite) may even don their
traditional costumes for parish festivities at the
Saint-Roch church.

Even with entertainment guides flooding the market, the celebrated Morris column continues to play a pivotal rôle in alerting the public to upcoming cultural events. Yet for those with a keen eye le spectacle *is everywhere to be seen: from the knife grinder on the Ile Saint-Louis to the roving accordionist in a remote 20th* arrondissement *courtyard.*

Public parks in the summer season where old and young alike find simple amusements and diversions. While adults listen to the traditional fanfare, wooden carousel horses rock tender youth to and fro... leaving the turbulence of bumper cars to hardier sorts (following page).

Jugglers, tumblers, showmen have no need for grand staircases or proscenium stage. Casual, improvised theatre returns to its origins on medieval paving stones capturing an unsuspecting crowd of passersby.

Seventeenth-century Paris... the Marais... and its heartbeat the Place des Vosges, the city's oldest square built on the instructions of Henri IV (1604). An oasis of tranquility in the center of town. An accordion wails, fountains splash, lovers embrace, reverie is in the air. The madding crowd is far from these echoing arcades. Humanity where are you? Where else but on the Champs-Elysées (following page), worshipping the champion cyclists of the Tour de France race.

Postcard Paris

Postcard Paris? I have personal experience of postcard Paris. There is a postcard tacked on the wall of my tiny *chambre de bonne*. A garret yes, with a sink, a bidet, very French windows, very romantic, often very cold. The card is in muted tones of brown and rose and is signed in script in the corner: *Lumière*. Booksellers on the *quais* of the River Seine, it says. And there is one old man with a white beard lifting the dark wooden lid of his bookstall, a dark tree beside him, the gray wall behind, the silver strip of river, and in the distance the pale stone bridge, the sun and the mist rising over the gas lamps. The quality of light is such that the photograph could have been taken yesterday, or could be an artist's rendition of 17th century booksellers setting up shop.

The postcard comes from my first trip as a wide-eyed Europe-on-the-run student seven years ago. I bought it at a shop just off the Place du Tertre, in Montmartre.

Three years later I found the same shop and the same card and the bearded bookseller in the picture seemed like a long-lost old friend. Now I live not far from the booksellers' *quai* and sometimes I walk the river at dawn looking for that old man, that image. And I've come very close. It's not real of course, but it is beautiful.

Postcard Paris? Paris France. City of Light. April in Paris. "I love Paris in the Springtime..." Balzac... and Rodin's magnificent statue of him. Proust. Victor Hugo. "The Hunchback of Notre-Dame." "A Tale of Two Cities." Madame Defarge knitting the Revolution together. Marie-Antoinette on her way to the guillotine. Napoleon, one hand always holding his heart.

The Eiffel Tower. What *was* the symbol of Paris before Monsieur E. Gustave Eiffel, designed this universal erector-set, dream piece for the *Exposition Universelle* of 1889? Called then a monstrosity, a "modern tower of Babel"... this tower is a marvelous torch that one looks for now, lit at night, and feels, yes, this is Paris.

Ride the big box elevator to the top early on in your visit, stand in the wind and look out over the panorama of vanilla buildings and cherry chimney tops, then you know, really know, yes, this is Paris.

Postcard Paris. Versailles and the hall of mirrors. Women in Empire décolletage. Men in silk, and powdered wigs, lace hankies up their sleeves. Lafayette to de Gaulle. The elegance of power. The power of elegance. The Arc de Triomphe. The parade of Liberation. GI Joes in Gay Paree. The Résistance. Somewhere an image of Clark Gable and Marlene Dietrich meeting in the rain. Brave. Pure. And then Pigalle (Pig Alley). A different kind of light. Neon. The enticements of "sin". Decadence and abandon. "Mademoiselle from Armentiers, parlez-vous?" To "Voulez-vous coucher avec moi?" Lovers on every corner. Lovers kissing under the bridges that cross the Seine. The placid, romantic Seine. The fishermen on the *quais*. The "hippies" on the banks. The Bateaux-Mouches gliding swanlike past coal barges. The bridges arching gracefully from Right Bank to Left.

Postcard Paris. The Latin Quarter. The student quarter. The Sorbonne. Another brief encounter with gargoyles leaning out into the alleys from St. Severin. The narrow, cobbled streets. St. Michel. May '68. The *Boul' Mich'*. Beaux Arts students in fall. A lean boy in jeans, black scarf thrown around his neck, a small frizzy-haired, kohl-eyed girl, their sketch pads under their arms. The garret artists come down to the river *quais* to sketch Notre-Dame.

Postcard Paris. Rushing to the Louvre to see Mona Lisa. The Louvre —world proclamation of superiority in all things "art". Cold palace, once home of the royal court: overwhelming, exhausting. Renoir. Better, the Jeu de Paume... Monet, Manet. Montmartre, Place du Tertre. The artists and easels grouped like a carnival. The bright blue sky. The bright red awnings of the cafés. Climbing the crooked mile to the bright, alabaster sanctuary of Sacré-Cœur. Pale but blinding light. Back down to Utrillo's Paris. The cafés of Toulouse-Lautrec. Baudelaire, Verlaine, and Rimbaud drinking absinthe. Dark light. The night light. The Folies.

Paris' passing fads. Fashions that leave an indelible stamp. Feathers and champagne. Joséphine Baker. Charles Boyer: "Ah, yes, I raymember eet well." Edith Piaf, sparrow of the streets. The smoky jazz clubs. The "caves". Django Reinhart, Sidney Béchet. Blue smoke. Black skin. Golden saxophone. Young Belmondos in Borsolino slouch hats. St. Germain des Prés. Juliette Gréco. Young girls in poney tails and black turtleneck sweaters. Simone and Sartre. The existentialist cafés. Giacometti. Malraux. Politics and art. The importance of being intellectual over café and calvados.

Postcard Paris. An American in Paris. Hemingway's moveable feast, Henry Miller's black spring. Anais Nin taking it all down, taking it all in. Gertrude Stein and Alice B. holding court, holding forth. Picasso. The war in Spain. The war at home. The war for democracy. The war with words. The war between form and content. Breaking up formal sentence structure Breaking out of old philosophies, out of the canvas, out in song. Caussimon standing on the table at *Lapin Agile* back up in Montmartre. Marx and Lenin having wine and cheese at La Tartine. All the exiles. The runaway aristocracy. The political refugees.

Postcard Paris. The Americans who came not to be F. Scott Fitzgeralded "The rich are different from you and me." So are the French, but one could be poor in Paris and live on light. Though one often forgets, Hemingway was killing pigeons, stoning them in Luxembourg Garden, for dinner.

There is some wonderful agreement here between architecture and light to please you, to soothe you, to surprise you. With secret fountains. With window boxes of flowers. With the wrinkled old face of a concierge behind the courtyard door. A procession of schoolchildren with knapsack schoolbags strapped on their backs. Windows. Chimneys. Cobbled alleyways and old stone houses that pick up the sun and hold it all day, transforming from clean white to mellow yellow, to romantic rose on a clear day, staying stately, firmly, formally 18th century gray on others.

For absolutely no *centimes* a day or for the price of a postcard, you can follow the gleam of the golden dome of the Opera, wonder what bargains are struck between exiled Counts and flowergirl waifs at the nearby Café de la Paix. Stroll the high price boutiques: Chanel, St. Laurent, Hermès.

Fashion, there is always fashion. Style is all here. And, yes the women *are* beautiful.

The women of *Crazy Horse* dress in light only, or almost. The Irma La Douce of the Halles works in daylight. Les Halles. Onion soup and rich red wine. Broadbacked men in white butcher aprons opening the market at dawn. It's gone now. It's called the hole now. But even here the reality of modernization, or La Défense skyscraperdom, doesn't intrude for long. There will always be Les Halles in our heads. And there are other markets, so many other magical markets. Real food. No plastic.

Postcard Paris changes, but remains the same. Restored *Place des Vosges:* a fold-out children's storybook, ringed with doll's house seventeenth century mansions. It comes as a shock perhaps that there is no Bastille. But there is a winged victory perched on a column and a smaller statue of liberty at the Pont de Grenelle. Paris. Place de la Concorde. Concorde: a sleek half-French bird, high speed, high class, high priced, but oh what style.

The images remain as constant as postcards. We all know them. The exiles. The expatriates. The artists. The farmers in Iowa know them. They are what Paris is. And those exiles, artists, and farmers come to Paris, to visit or to stay, because they are fascinated with romantic images or with the postcard concept of *liberté, égalité, fraternité.* They tour the monuments. They sit in cafés. Sometimes they are hungry and sometimes an impeccable penguin waiter will be nasty to them in a language they don't understand and which no longer sounds like a language that makes even "take out the garbage" sound lyrical, and it doesn't matter really. Because those romantic, postcard images always win out. They are stronger, than reality. They are seen through a light that is difficult to describe.

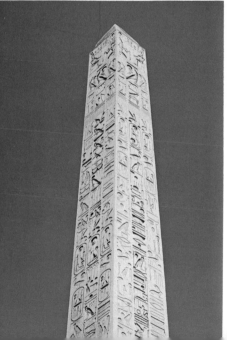

*Parisians at work and at play.
A waiter at Fouquet's on the
Champs-Elysées (top left) hopes
to find a tip on the table he's
clearing. A cook from the
bustling Beaux-Arts restaurant
(bottom left) takes time out for a
family chat while workmen
surrounded by the aura of
Napoleonic victory (opposite)
play to win at a game of boules
(a national pastime) during
lunch hour in the Tuileries.*

Leisurely life on the river banks: a burst of blossoms along the quay's Marché aux Fleurs (top left) inaugurated (like so much else) by Napoleonic decree in 1809... booksellers peddle their oddities to rummaging customers looking for the find amidst attic castaways... amateur and professional artists take to the bridges to find a new angle for an age-old subject.

Not only Parisians inhabit Paris.   Flocks of birds have been granted their place by Parisians willing to put up with their occasional insolence for the mere pleasure of hearing them twitter in the few surviving trees... even going so far as to accept their winged ridicule of the most solemn statues as long as they'll flutter down for a feed in the hand.

The Seine is still a great artery of navigation, as it was in the Middle Ages. Sightseeing cruisers like the famous Bateaux Mouche make heavy use of the waterway during the peak seasons... barges transport heavy cargoes while others, converted into houseboats, are permanently moored along the banks. Aquatic rhythms set the pace; the mood is one of dolce farniente and life is lived in slow motion with the automobile finally silenced on the barge deck. Swept up in this lazy atmosphere, the bookseller lets out a simian yawn.

Under the Panthéon's dome (top left) are buried some of France's most famous dead. Here lie the venerable bones of Jean-Jacques Rousseau, Victor Hugo, Mirabeau, Voltaire, Zola and many others. Domes and cupolas breaking the horizon's monotony. Variations on a theme of centuries from burnished helmet to Panthéon to Invalides (both top left) to Institut de France (opposite).

La Butte-Montmartre, Sacré-Cœur... one of Paris' outlying villages (still a commune libre) *which has most carefully preserved its rural character and characters. Though its celebrated artists' colony has long since dispersed to Saint-Germain and Montparnasse, the ever picturesque Butte remains a haven for free spirits, modern-day torch bearers of* la vie de bohème.

The age of Art Nouveau lives on through the many surviving Métro station entrances designed by Hector Guimard in 1900 for the Paris Métro Company. These metal structures so typified the curled, skeletal qualities of Art Nouveau, that the whole movement was popularly know as "Style Métro". A descent into the Métro's

*subterranean stations guarantees entertainment
from busking bands and improvising showmen of
all sorts... like the clown below caught napping
between numbers.   Following double page:
Twilight captured on the quays through the eye
of a poet? painter? sitting under the Pont des
Arts across the river from the Louvre.*

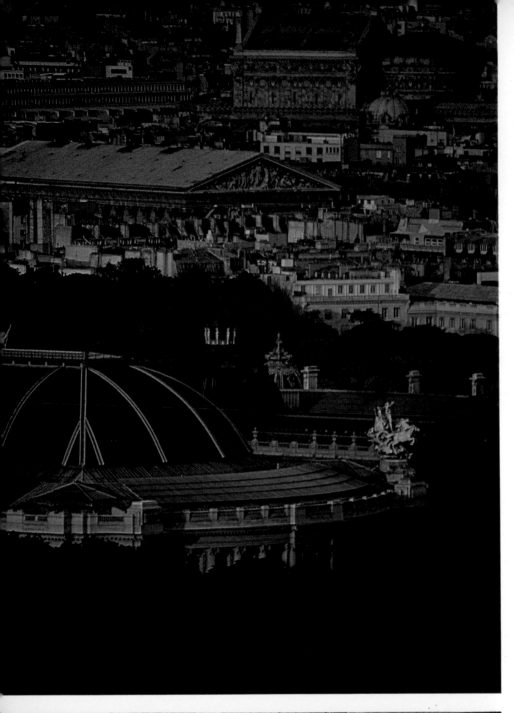

The sun sets on a city casting a luminous rose-colored glow on familiar facades — the Grand Palais, the Madeleine, the Opera, Place Vendôme (all top left). A warmth and luminosity so beautifully Parisian like the municipal police band blowing their horns or an elderly citizen escaping solitude in a public garden. Day slips into dusk.

As twilight glimmers across a silhouetted sky, the City of Light takes up her torch, illuminating the way for the biggest spectacle of them all: Paris by night. Imperceptibly night falls and more lights and lanterns begin to flicker sending the weary home and luring the fauna out. Following double page: Three ghostly nuns cross the Place de la Concorde.

Razzle dazzle neon night life. Glitter, glamour,
sex, sophistication, splish and splash. Crazy
nights at the Crazy Horse (following double
page) with Vanilla Banana,
Polly Underground, Greta Fahrenheit...

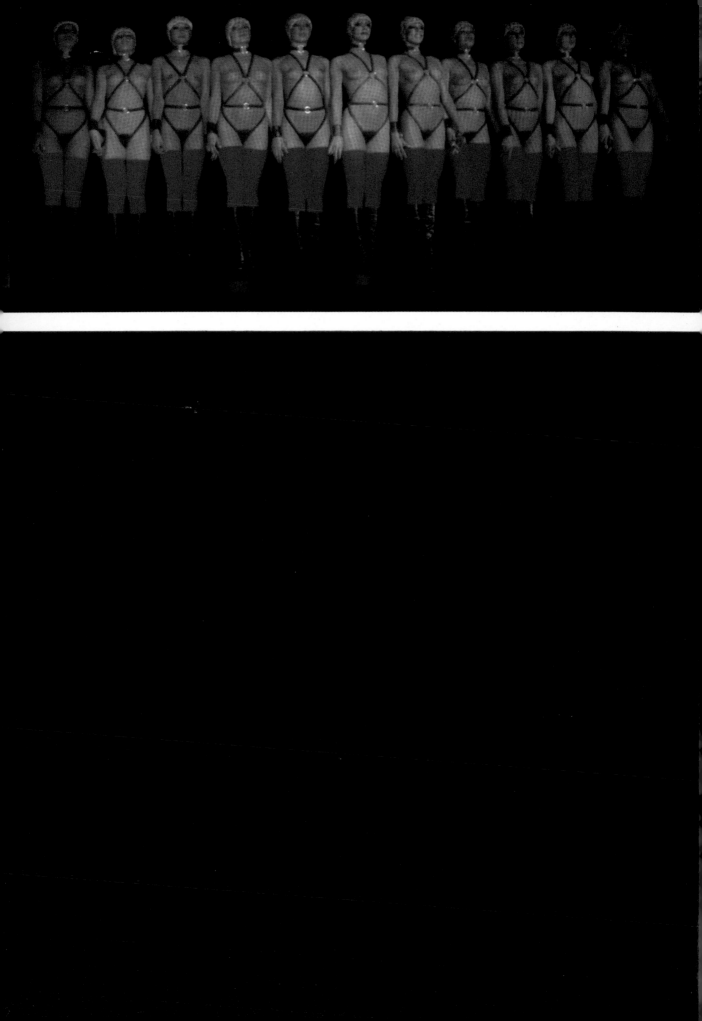

The great Parisian Music Hall tradition is still
kicking up its heels — whether rowdy can-can or
sophisticated striptease. A throbbing daytime
metropolis slips into something comfortable and
turns the lights on, not out. The long day's
journey into night is well on its way to dawn.

A love-hate affair

Here it comes—every Parisian's 19th nervous breakdown...

"I'm sick of Paris. I tell you. I can't stand it any more. The cars. The pollution. All that dust and noise. It's unhealthy. The people are artificial.

"You never know what they are thinking. What they are trying to get out of you. They are sarcastic and unfriendly. Always making personal remarks and snap judgements. I'll find a way, I'm sure of it. I'll move to the country. I will!"

It never fails. At the onset of their month-long summer vacations, Parisians agree, for once. They forget their *café*-table arguments and quibbles. The staunchest of city types joins the consensus: they all want out. Yet, a month later. Fresh and tanned. They are back at the Gare de Lyon, swinging their suitcases with *hop-là!* excitement. Resolute as lemmings.

Paris is a capital is a capital. A capital with splendid monuments and quiet cloisters. With elegant, formal parks and quaint, secret gardens.

Paris is a cultural center. An international city. With victory arches. Fortresses. Grand, commanding avenues. A city planned to be beautiful. Designed to be stunning by its rulers, (Charles V, François 1er, Louis XV, Napoléon I and III...), schemed and planned by its nobles and politicians, (Maurice de Sully, Richelieu, Mazurin, Colbert), given its grandeur by favored architects (Haussmann, Chalgrin...). But which still holds secrets, surprises like the charming, private courtyards and unexpected *impasses,* narrow, dead-ends, which give the city it's *cachet,* stamp, originality, charm.

Paris is a city that survives on an impressive, romantic past and wears itself out living dangerously in hot pursuit of passing fads. Bang on, right now.

Paris is the capital of protest. First to plunge into *mouvements sociaux,* Parisian euphamism for strike action and public demonstrations. A bastion of male chauvinism, where Women's Lib, has nevertheless gained a strong foothold.

Paris is youth and age, change and tradition. Paris has many faces. Paris could be... the wrinkled features of an old lady dressed in partial-mourning. Black pullover. Sober-cut gray flannel coat. Silver hair severely drawn back in a neatly pinned *chignon,* bun. Choosing a chicken *bien ferme,* nice and firm, for the day her grandchild comes to lunch. Paris could be... an alternative *Parisienne,* the scatty, frizzy-locked young girl sporting a moth-eaten, flea-market acquired fur coat, bargain hunting at the Marché Saint-Pierre cloth market, near the Sacré-Cœur.

Paris is a trendy, bustling city attached to its anachronisms, archaïsms and incongruities. A capital.

Photography and design **Bernard Hermann**
Text edited by **Georgina Oliver**
of "Paris-Metro"
Printed in Japan by Zokeisha Publishing Co.
First published: March 1978
Publisher's N°: 83